All Ri

MW01242996

Adam Gasiewski and Hiba Atif.

Days Without Sex

This book is dedicated to Elon Musk, Barack Obama, and Jahseh Onfroy.

Days Without Sex

Days Without Sex…

Compiled by Adam Gasiewski and Hiba Atif

Day 0 without sex:

Life fucks me every day

@Dalton_AFarrier

Day 1 without sex:

Beginning to feel my
virginity coming back

@Sergiowtd

Day 2 without sex:

Went to an airport, put drugs in my pocket just so I could get patted down...I didn't even have a flight.

@Lovely68mary

Day 3 without sex:

I think I'm losing
hearing in my left eye

@OhShxtDatsVar

Day 4 without sex:

I spit on my popsicle before putting it in my mouth

@Erkiebear

Day 5 without sex:

Went to Taco Bell and told the hot employee my name was daddy

@Asap_Bandz1

Day 6 without sex:

Asked a mosquito to land on my ass so I could justify spanking myself

@MyolLife

Day 8 without sex:

I was driving and decided to slam on my brakes just so someone could hit me from the back

@CandyCity_Chick

Day 26 without sex:

I let my hair get caught in my truck door so something would pull it

@efranklin013

Day 29 without sex:

Went bowling just so
I could finger something

@_Darthandrew

Day 42 without sex:

This is my second time being tattooed in 5 days so someone will touch my thigh

@LilyMichellee

Day 50 without sex:

Just fainted while
stirring mac & cheese

@vinnybrack

Day 53 without sex:

Went to the beach today just so the waves could smack my ass

@sarahcrispy_

Day 57 without sex:

I went to the beach and a crab pinched my ass and I asked him to do it again

@biancagarcia_

Day 58 without sex:

I went under the speed limit so I could feel how it felt to have my ass rode again

@alexismarie21__

Day 67 without sex:

Went to Six Flags so I could remember what it was like to ride and scream

@_aquinoleslie

Day 69 without sex:

Nice. But also not nice

@SJSchauer

Day 71 without sex:

My smart watch
thinks I've jogged 3 miles
today but I haven't left
the house

@m_cGuire

Day 87 without sex:

Purposely drove on the side of the highway so the rumble strip would make my car vibrate

@brookexsaunders

Day 98 without sex:

I ate two Popeyes biscuits without water so it could choke me

@ItsThatOneGuy88

Day 111 without sex:

I let out a small moan when I slid my bank card inside the ATM machine

@LowkeyChanice

Day 136 without sex:

Went to church for the first time in a long time because I wanted to remember how it was to be on my knees

@DamarisRobless

Day 147 without sex:

Ate fruit gushers so I could feel something squirt in my mouth

@Kaitlyn_Ross97

Day 152 without sex:

When my grandmother told me to shut up I bit my lip and said make me

@victorbruz

Day 173 without sex:

Got arrested just to feel what it's like to get hit on and have the cuffs on my hands again

@EliteEmir

Day 175 without sex:

I only shaved one leg so when I lay in bed and my legs rub against each other, it feels like I'm laying next to a man

@Daddyissues__

Day 176 without sex:

I gagged on my toothbrush and liked it

@uhnyluhh

Day 196 without sex:

I went to the market to get a watermelon and got a little turned on slapping it trying to see if it was a good one

@The RealMikeskee

Day 213 without sex:

Plugged my charger into my phone and whispered "you like that?"

@allen88_d

Day 231 without sex:

Put a bowl of jello on my stomach just so I can see something jiggle on top of me

@BroderickHunter

Day 236 without sex:

Got a job as a plumber so I could feel what it's like to lay pipe again

@DavidAlvareeezy

Day 243 without sex:

I suck on my vape
for a few seconds longer
so something will choke
me

@keightyrose

Day 244 without sex:

I put the vacuum
hose on my neck so it
could give me a hickey

@kennedyaleman2

Day 274 without sex:

My sleep paralysis demon is starting to look kinda thicc

@Pissedoffhotdog

Day 275 without sex:

I just played Fortnite to remember what it's like to get fucked

@Isaiahfromny

Day 278 without sex:

I made Siri call me daddy

@AdrianDiaz250

Day 283 without sex:

A mosquito sucked on my neck and I moaned a little bit

@ClifSosa

Day 284 without sex:

I just rubbed my own thigh and asked myself "So what you trynna do"

@ThegodPreston

Day 298 without sex:

Considering asking the FBI agent in my camera for ass pics

@paulito

Day 321 without sex:

My momma whooped my ass today with a belt and I accidentally moaned. We're currently not speaking

@sebasyuh

Day 329 without sex:

I went to Starbucks just so I could hear somebody scream my name

@ryankii

Day 357 without sex:

I just texted myself "wyd" at 2 am

@PonyBoy__1

Day 362 without sex:

I moaned while cleaning my ears with a Q-tip

@chuck33hl

Day 365 without sex:

My bathing suit going up my ass kinda turns me on

@yagurlleal

Day 425 without sex:

I stand outside in the rain just to feel wet

@edwiinali

Day 436 without sex:

My priest said I will
be punished for my sins I
said yes daddy thank you

@gretafromspace

Day 475 without sex:

The crack in my couch cushions looking kinda cute

@trandat_

Day 476 without sex:

I'm jealous of this storm bc even the thunder is clapping and my cheeks aren't

@jess_nunley7

Day 613 without sex:

I unplugged my charger from my phone just so I could remember the feeling of pulling out

@erap_ejercito

Day 652 without sex:

I tried kissing my
own neck

@saradesdinn

Day 678 without sex:

Someone said "who's a good girl" at the dog park and I said "me daddy"

@taylorblaisee

Day 679 without sex:

I have conversations with people that don't brush their teeth, just so someone can talk dirty to me

@anishsidda

Day 726 without sex:

I bought a Boston cream donut on my way to work this morning because I forgot what it was like to get creamed in my mouth

@L_A_B__

Day 835 without sex:

I only use a straw so
I have something to suck

@Bradley28_

Day 918 without sex:

I tail whipped my ankle with a scooter on purpose just to feel something

@Olivertree

Day 1415 without sex:

Went to school to become a cop so I could handcuff myself

@snl4me

Day 1738 without sex:

Threw the blue shell in Mario Kart while I was already in first place to remember what it's like to get hit from behind

@john_silcox

Day 6987 without sex:

Idk I'm still a virgin

@GarvenKamryn

Acknowledgements

We'd like to thank Rachel G. Stark (@ragsisme) for suggesting this brilliant book idea, as well as all of the fantastic Twitter users who came up with these hilarious tweets. Please go check them out and give. Them. Some. LIIKKEEESSSS!!!

Follow Us!!

Hiba Atif

@thenameshiba

Adam Gasiewski

@adam_gasiewski

21006875R00037

Made in the USA
Lexington, KY
08 December 2018